Teaching Healthy Cooking and Nutrition

in Primary Schools, Book 4

Cheesy Bread, Apple Crumble, Chilli con Carne and Other Recipes

Sandra Mulvany

Brilliant
PUBLICATIONS

We hope you and your pupils enjoy trying out the recipes in this book and learning about healthy eating. Brilliant Publications publishes many other books to help primary school teachers. To find out more details on all of our titles, including those listed below, please log onto our website: www.brilliantpublications.co.uk.

Other titles in the Teaching Healthy Cooking and Nutrition in Primary Schools series:

Other titles published by Brilliant Publications

Published by Brilliant Publications
Unit 10,
Sparrow Hall Farm,
Edlesborough,
Dunstable,
Bedfordshire,
LU6 2ES

www.brilliantpublications.co.uk

The name Brilliant Publications
and the logo are registered trade marks.

Written by Sandra Mulvany
Illustrated by Kerry Ingham
Cover design by Brilliant Publications
Photography by Brilliant Publications
Printed in the UK

Printed ISBN 978-1-78317-111-8
e-book ISBN 978-1-78317-117-0

The first edition of this book, published in 2008, had the title: Healthy Cooking for Primary Schools, Book 4. This second edition was first printed and published in the UK in 2014

10 9 8 7 6 5 4 3 2 1

Contents

Contents (cont.)

Introduction and Links to the National Curriculum

The *Teaching Healthy Cooking and Nutrition in Primary Schools* series is a practical school programme for schools. It focuses on the progression in cooking skills through easy-to-follow recipes. Essential cooking skills, theory and health and safety points are introduced progressively throughout the series.

The programme is designed to teach pupils practical cooking whilst incorporating the theory into the hands-on activity. Each of the five books in the series contains 12 recipes, together with visual lesson structure cards, visual learning objectives and photographs of the food – all of which are photocopiable.

All the recipes are presented in two formats, one laid out in a traditional way and one in a visual step-by-step format, enabling the recipes to be used with pupils of all ages or with groups with differing reading abilities. It is recommended that, after a cooking session, the recipes are photocopied and sent home with pupils, so that children can try making the recipes at home.

There are two assessment sheets in the book (on pages 85–86). The assessment sheets test and reinforce the practical and theoretical knowledge gained. You will also find a photocopiable certificate on page 87 for when pupils have completed all the tasks.

This second edition of *Teaching Healthy Cooking and Nutrition in Primary Schools* has been amended to ensure that it addresses the requirements of the National Curriculum for England (September 2014). The programmes of study state that pupils should be taught how to cook and apply the principles of nutrition and healthy eating. It aims to instil in pupils a love of cooking and to teach them a life skill that will enable pupils to feed themselves and others affordably and well, now and in later life.

Key Stage 1 pupils should be taught to use the basic principles of a healthy and varied diet to prepare dishes and understand where food comes from.

Key Stage 2 pupils should be taught to:
- understand and apply the principles of a healthy and varied diet
- prepare and cook a variety of predominantly savoury dishes using a range of cooking techniques
- understand seasonality, and know where and how a variety of ingredients are grown, reared, caught and processed.

The series also links well with the Health and Wellbeing section of the Scottish Curriculum for Excellence and the Guidance on the Schools (Health Promotion and Nutrition) (Scotland) Act 2007.

How to Use the Resources

All ingredients are based on two pupils sharing, and the timings will all fit into a double lesson of approximately 80 minutes. We recommend you use low-fat options where possible.

Make a display using the Visual Lesson Structure Cards (pages 7–10) and pictures of the recipe and skill to be focussed on in the lesson (colour versions of the photographs can be downloaded from the Brilliant Publications' website).

Keep the skill, theory and health and safety point sheets to hand so that you can refer to them when demonstrating to pupils. (The language has been kept as simple as possible on these sheets, so you may wish to give copies to your pupils as well.)

Choose the best format of the recipe to use for each pair of children and photocopy sufficient copies. The illustrated versions of the recipes can be photocopied onto either an A3 sheet (if space is an issue, fold it in half so that you view six steps at a time), or reduced to A4 size.

If you place the recipes and other sheets in clear plastic wallets (or laminate them), they can be used again and again.

Encourage children to gather together all the ingredients and equipment they need before starting. They could tick things off on their copy of the recipe.

Demonstrate the recipe 2–3 steps at a time, introducing the skill, theory and health and safety points as you progress through the recipe.

An important aspect of learning to cook is learning to work together. You may wish to display the Discussion cards on pages 11–12 (Communicate, Share, Help, Be pleasant) so that you can refer to these throughout the lesson.

The assessment sheets on pages 85 and 86 provide a fun way of testing the practical and theoretical knowledge gained. The Certificate of Achievement on page 87 can either be used as an ongoing record or be given out when all the recipes in the book have been completed.

On pages 88–89 there is a chart giving some suggestions for adapting the recipes for children with allergies and intolerances, and/or religious and lifestyle considerations. None of the recipes use nuts. Before you start any cooking activities, you should send home a letter asking parents to inform you if there are any allergy/lifestyle/religious considerations that you need to take into account. You may need to follow this up with a letter or phone call to clarify any issues raised. A useful chart listing some religious food customs can be found at: www.childrensfoodtrust.org.uk/assets/the-standards/3food-customs.pdf.

Above all, have fun and enjoy cooking!

Today We are Making

1

Today We are Learning

2

Read Recipe

3

Wash Hands and Prepare

4

Cook

5

Clear Away

6

Tasting

7

We Have Learnt

8

Communicate

It is vital to have good communication in a cooking environment. If you are working with a partner, it is important to say what you are doing and to agree on who does what. You have to talk about what you would like to do and listen to what your partner wants to do. Then you have to work out a way to make it fair for both of you. You can only come to an agreement if you talk together!

You should also let others know if there are any dangers, such as you opening the oven or if water has been spilt on the floor. Talking is absolutely key to good cooking habits. The better you are at communicating, the better you are at cooking in a school environment.

Share

Good sharing follows on from good communicating. If you have communicated well, you will have reached a fair decision about sharing. Sharing works best when it has been done fairly and everyone is happy. Sharing is particularly difficult if it involves doing something really exciting or really boring. You have to imagine that the other person feels very much like yourself. This can be hard to imagine, but it is an important lesson to learn. Sharing is a lot easier when you talk together about things.

Help

It is important to be able to help others, but it is also important to accept help from others. Help is a two-way thing. If you are offering your help to someone else, it is important that you choose your words carefully. Be kind in giving your help, as it can be hard to accept help given with harsh words. If you have communicated well, you will be able to help each other well. If you are very capable, offer your help kindly, but also let others help you in return, even if it is to do with something you feel you might already know about.

Be pleasant

It is, in fact, very simple to be pleasant. Look at and listen to the person you are working with and notice something he or she does well. Then say something pleasant about that. You will soon discover that the more pleasant you are to people, the more pleasant they are back to you. You can also do something pleasant, like smile at a person or pat someone kindly on the back. Don't just wait for someone to be pleasant to you; try to be the first one to say or do something pleasant.

Cheesy Bread with Rosemary

How to Shape Bread Rolls

You can shape buns in any way that you want. However, one good way is to first divide the dough into equal sizes, then shape the pieces into balls, pulling dough edges under to make a smooth top. This makes for a pretty and smooth bun that you can brush with egg.

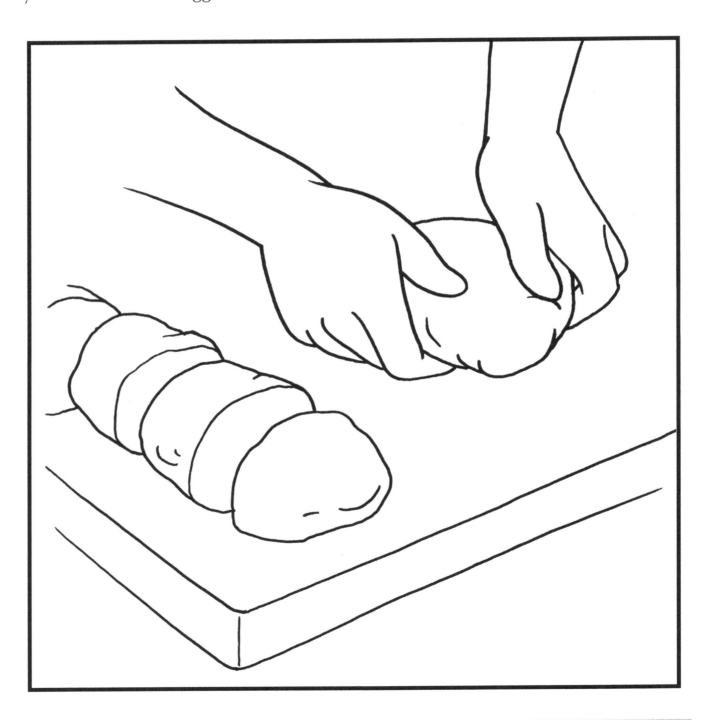

Smell and Looks are Important

We eat with all our senses. It is not just important how food tastes; it is also very important what food looks like and how it smells. Before we get to taste any food, we will have formed an opinion about it, based on looks and smell. So, the smell and look of food is much more important than you might think.

Be Aware of Additives

Additives, such as colourings, preservatives, antioxidants or sweeteners, are often used in mass-produced foods. This is done to enhance the look, taste or, in particular, shelf-life of food. In Europe, all recognized additives are given a name, and they all begin with E (For example, E100 is Curcumin, a colouring used in fish fingers). E-numbers are very controversial. Many people believe that E-numbers are a contributing factor to hyperactivity in children as well as to allergies and even cancer. In any case, E-numbers mean that the food is no longer just made of natural products.

Cheesy Bread with Rosemary

Ingredients: 250g strong white flour   1 tsp margarine
1 sachet yeast   50g Cheddar cheese   Water
2 tsp dried rosemary   1 egg

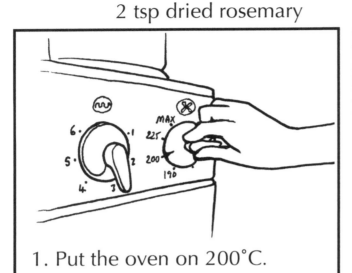

1. Put the oven on 200°C.

2. Put flour in a bowl.

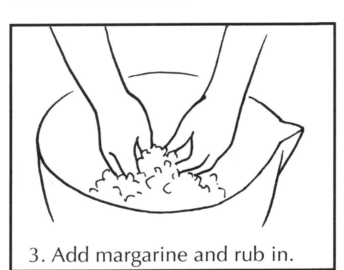

3. Add margarine and rub in.

4. Add the yeast and rosemary and mix.

5. Grate the cheese.

6. Add the cheese and mix.

Cheesy Bread with Rosemary (cont.)

Equipment:

	Mixing bowl	Cup	Whisk/fork
Brush	Mixing spoon	Teaspoon	Grater
Measuring jug	Flour dredger	Scales	Baking tray

Recipe

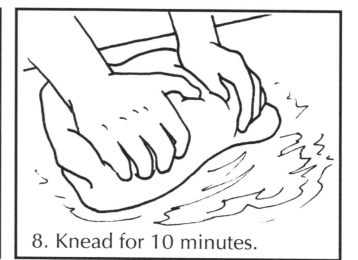

7. Add enough lukewarm water to form a dough.

8. Knead for 10 minutes.

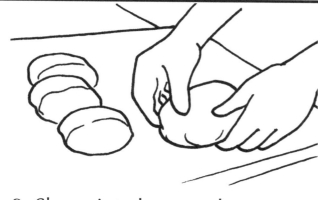

9. Shape into buns and put on a baking tray.

10. Crack an egg into a cup and whisk.

11. Brush the buns with the egg.

12. Bake in the oven for 10–15 minutes.

Recipe

Cheesy Bread with Rosemary

Ingredients:
250g strong white flour
50g Cheddar cheese
1 sachet yeast
1 tsp margarine
Water
2 tsp dried rosemary
1 egg

Equipment:
Mixing bowl
Cup
Whisk/fork
Brush
Mixing spoon
Teaspoon
Grater

Measuring jug
Flour dredger
Scales
Baking tray

Instructions:

1.   Put the oven on 200°C.

2.   Put flour in a bowl.

3.   Add margarine and rub in.

4.   Add the yeast and rosemary and mix.

5.   Grate the cheese.

6.   Add the cheese and mix.

7.   Add enough lukewarm water to form a dough.

8.   Knead for 10 minutes.

9.   Shape into buns and put on a baking tray.

10.   Crack an egg into a cup and whisk.

11.   Brush the buns with the egg.

12.   Bake in the oven for 10–15 minutes.

Savoury Rolls

How to Use a Pastry Brush

It is easy and fun to use a brush in cooking. You can brush some breads and cakes with egg. The brushing will give the bread or cake a shiny finish that will look attractive. There are also other reasons for brushing. Sometimes you brush edges of dough to seal two edges together like glue. Other times the brushing may act as glue for sesame seeds sprinkled on top. If you do not have egg, you can use milk.

What is a Vegetarian?

A vegetarian is a person who does not eat any meat or fish. "Vegans" are even stricter, as they do not eat anything that comes from animals, such as dairy products, eggs or honey. People choose to become vegetarians or vegans for different reasons, either personal, cultural, religious or environmental.

How do Vegetarians Replace Lost Nutrients?

Vegetarians cut out meat from their diet. This means that vegetarians lose out on an important source of nutrients, in particular, protein. Proteins are vital to the body for growth and repair. Some proteins can be produced by the body, but at least eight amino acids (the building blocks of protein) have to come from what we eat. A protein which contains all the essential amino acids is called a "complete protein". Foods from animal sources contain complete proteins. Most plant foods are "incomplete" because they are missing one or more of the essential amino acids. Therefore you need to eat a variety of plant-based proteins to get all the essential amino acids.

Savoury Rolls

Ingredients: 125g wholemeal flour   60g margarine
1 egg   2 tbsp cold water   Stuffing mix

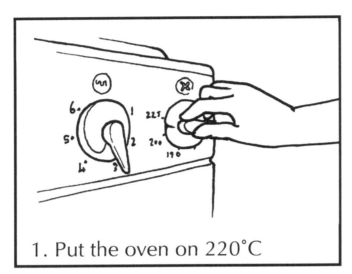

1. Put the oven on 220°C

2. Put flour in a bowl.

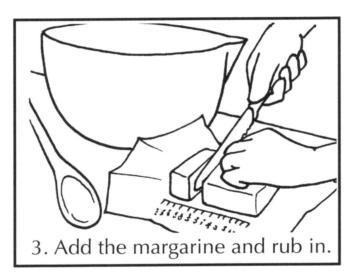

3. Add the margarine and rub in.

4. Add water to form dough.

5. Roll out pastry to a rectangle.
   Cut into 2 strips.

6. Prepare the stuffing.

Savoury Rolls (cont.)

Equipment:

Scales	Mixing bowl	Whisk	Mixing spoon
Baking tray	Brush	Knife	Tablespoon
	Flour dredger	Cup	Rolling pin

7. Put the stuffing down the centre of the strips.

8. Crack an egg into a cup and whisk.

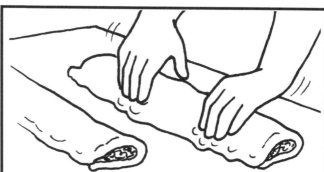

9. Brush the edges with egg.

10. Fold the pastry over the stuffing and press edges together.

11. Cut into rolls, put on baking tray and brush with egg

12. Bake for 10 minutes.

Teaching Healthy Cooking and Nutrition, Book 4

Recipe

Savoury Rolls

Ingredients:
125g wholemeal flour
60g margarine
1 egg
2 tbsp cold water
Stuffing mix

Equipment:
Mixing bowl
Whisk
Mixing spoon
Scales
Brush
Knife
Tablespoon
Baking tray
Flour dredger
Cup
Rolling pin

Instructions:

1. Put the oven on 220°C.

2. Put flour in a bowl.

3. Add the margarine and rub in.

4. Add water to form dough.

5. Roll out pastry to a rectangle. Cut into 2 strips.

6. Prepare the stuffing.

7. Put the stuffing down the centre of the strips.

8. Crack an egg into a cup and whisk.

9. Brush the edges with egg.

10. Fold the pastry over the stuffing and press edges together

11. Cut into rolls, put on baking tray and brush with egg.

12. Bake for 10 minutes.

Apple Crumble

How to Core an Apple

You can use a tool called an apple corer to press through the middle of the apple and thereby core the apple. However, this can be very dangerous, as you may easily lose your grip. A much safer way is to use a sharp knife and cut all four sides off the apple, thereby leaving the core in the middle. Once you have cut the first side off, you can place this flat side down and cut the next side off, turning it and cutting the next side off and so on. Be careful when cutting the first side, however, as a round apple is unsteady.

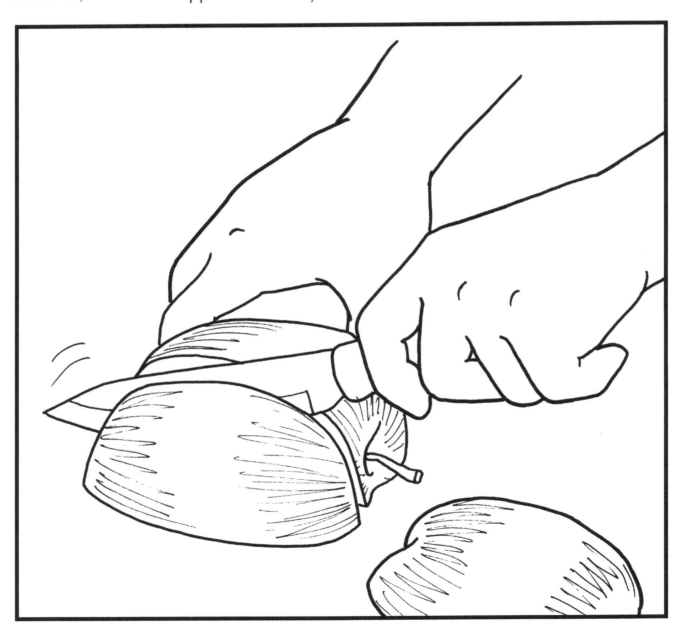

Why Do Apples Go Brown?

How can it be avoided?

Apples contain enzymes that react with the oxygen in the air. This makes the apple go brown when you cut it. It is called enzymatic browning. You can slow down the browning by inactivating the enzyme with heat (cooking the apple), sprinkling with lemon juice (the vitamin C acts as an antioxidant) or reducing the amount of available oxygen (putting the apple pieces in water).

Setting Knives Down Safely

Always lay knives down flat and away from the edge of the table.

Always be aware of where your sharp knife is! When you are not using it, it must lie flat on the table and point away from the edge of the table where you are. This is for safety reasons. If you do not need the knife anymore, remove it from the table. If you put it ready to be washed, the same applies: it must lie flat and point away from the edge of the table.

Recipe

Apple Crumble

Ingredients:

1 apple   Lemon juice 75g wholemeal flour

50g margarine 25g oats   25g muscovado sugar

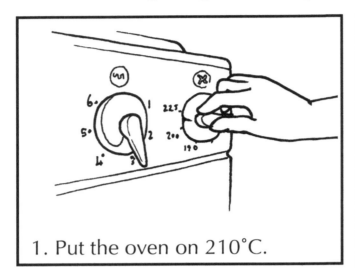

1. Put the oven on 210°C.

2. Put flour in a mixing bowl.

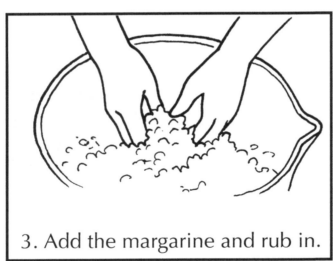

3. Add the margarine and rub in.

4. Add the sugar and mix.

5. Add the oats and mix.

6. Wash the apple and dry it.

Apple Crumble (cont.)

Recipe

Equipment:

Mixing bowl   Mixing spoon   Scales   Sharp knife
Chopping board   Dish   Baking tray

7. Core the apple.

8. Cut the apple into small pieces and put in a dish.

9. Sprinkle with lemon juice.

10. Pour the flour mixture over.

11. Place dish on a baking tray.

12. Bake for 15–20 minutes.

Teaching Healthy Cooking and Nutrition, Book 4

www.brilliantpublications.co.uk

Skill

Apple Crumble

Ingredients:
1 apple
Lemon juice
75g wholemeal flour
50g margarine
25g oats
25g muscovado sugar

Equipment:
Mixing bowl
Mixing spoon
Scales
Sharp knife
Chopping board
Dish
Baking tray

Instructions:

1.   Put the oven on 210°C.

2.   Put flour in a mixing bowl.

3.   Add the margarine and rub in.

4.   Add the sugar and mix.

5.   Add the oats and mix.

6.   Wash the apple and dry it.

7.   Core the apple.

8.   Cut the apple into small pieces and put in a dish.

9.   Sprinkle with lemon juice.

10.   Pour the flour mixture over.

11.   Place dish on a baking tray.

12.   Bake for 15–20 minutes.

Cheese and Mushroom Tarts

Using Weights and Measures on Food Packaging

It is often helpful to make use of the weights and measurements on a food's packaging. Instead of weighing out 50g of cheese from a 200g pack, for example, you simply have to look at the pack and estimate a quarter. Some butter and margarine packaging has marks indicating every 25g. This is most useful when only a roughly accurate amount is necessary. But with certain ingredients, such as the raising agents (yeast, etc) used in bread making, you will need to be as accurate as possible when measuring them out.

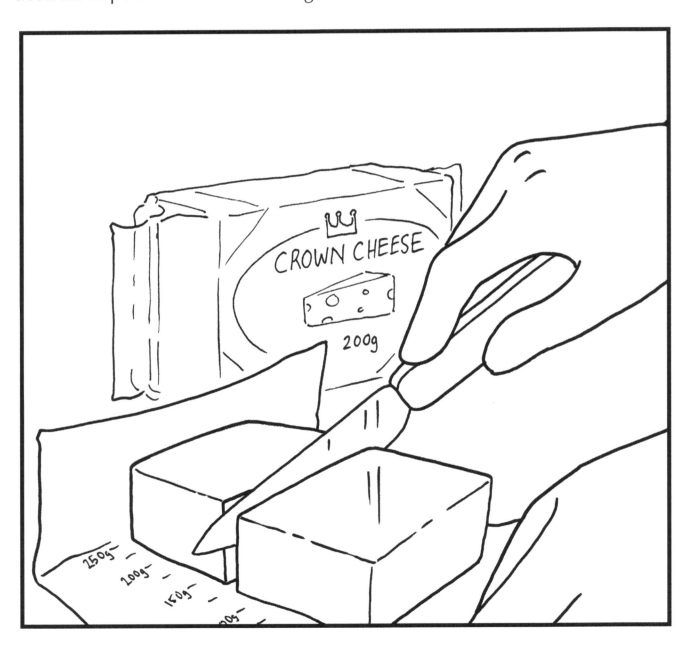

About Mushrooms

Edible mushrooms are healthy for you but never pick and eat any you find growing in the wild.

Edible mushrooms aren't just tasty, they're good for your health, too. They're low in fat and contain important minerals. What's more, they combine well with lots of different kinds of ingredients. The most common types of edible mushroom found in shops today are white cap, oyster and shitake. Supermarket bought mushrooms are commercially cultivated, so these mushrooms are available all-year-round.

Never eat wild mushrooms without advice from an expert, as there are many types of poisonous wild mushrooms.

Killing Bad Micro-organisms

There are several types of micro-organisms: bacteria, viruses, moulds and yeast. Not all are bad for us. In fact, we need yeast to help make beer and bread, and certain bacteria to help make cheeses, yogurt, sour cream and crème fraîche. However, many micro-organisms are bad for us and can cause food-related illnesses. To kill these micro-organisms, you have to cook food through thoroughly. Most micro-organisms multiply at temperatures between 5°C and 63°C. This is why food is refrigerated at below 5°C. Food should be cooked at a minimum of 70°C for at least 2 minutes to make sure that micro-organisms are destroyed. Even then you have to be careful.

Cheese and Mushroom Tarts

Ingredients: 60g wholemeal flour 30g margarine
1 egg 1–2 tbsp water 100ml milk
4 mushrooms 50g Cheddar cheese

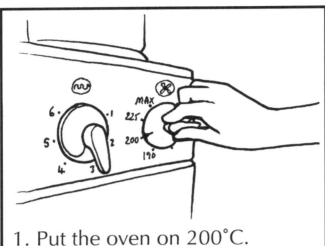

1. Put the oven on 200°C.

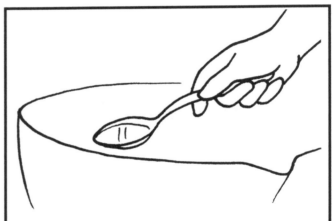

2. Weigh the flour and put in a bowl.

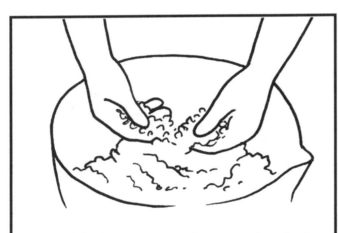

3. Add the margarine and rub in.

4. Add the water and form dough.

5. Sprinkle work surface with flour.

6. Roll out the pastry.

Cheese and Mushroom Tarts (cont.)

Recipe

Equipment: Mixing bowl   Whisk/fork   Mixing spoon
Sharp knife   2 pastry tins   Cup   Chopping board
Tablespoon   Flour dredger   Rolling pin Cheese grater   Scales

7. Line tins with pastry.

8. Crack an egg into a cup and whisk.

9. Add the milk and whisk.

10. Cut the mushrooms and grate the cheese. Add to tins.

11. Cover with egg mixture.

12. Bake in the oven for 20 minutes.

Teaching Healthy Cooking and Nutrition, Book 4
www.brilliantpublications.co.uk

Cheese and Mushroom Tarts

Ingredients:
60g wholemeal flour
30g margarine
1 egg
1–2 tbsp water
100ml milk
4 mushrooms
50g cheddar cheese

Equipment:
Mixing bowl
Whisk/fork
Mixing spoon
Sharp knife
2 pastry tins
Cup
Chopping board
Tablespoon

Flour dredger
Rolling pin
Cheese grater
Scales

Instructions:
1. Put the oven on 200°C.

2. Weigh the flour and put in a bowl.

3. Add the margarine and rub in.

4. Add the water and form dough.

5. Sprinkle work surface with flour.

6. Roll out the pastry.

7. Line tins with pastry.

8. Crack an egg into a cup and whisk.

9. Add the milk and whisk.

10. Cut the mushrooms and grate the cheese. Add to tins.

11. Cover with egg mixture.

12. Bake in the oven for 20 minutes.

Pizza Swirls

Skill

How to Flatten Slices

The way to flatten a slice, such as a pizza swirl or a cinnamon swirl, is to put the slice between your hands and press it gently but firmly. This will help to keep the swirl together during baking.

Strong Flour is Good for Bread Making

There are lots and lots of different types of flour. Plain flour, wholemeal flour, brown flour, strong white flour, self-raising flour and granary flour are amongst those most commonly used in baking. Strong flour is made from hard wheat and it is good for bread baking with yeast. This is because it contains a type of protein that forms gluten when mixed with water. The gluten is able to trap the carbon dioxide produced by the yeast and this makes the bread rise better. Therefore, the more gluten, the better for bread baking and this is why strong flour is good for bread baked with yeast.

Know the Emergency Numbers

Call 112 or 999. Both numbers are correct.

The emergency number is now 112. This is because it is the emergency number in other EU countries and Great Britain is part of the EU. You can still use 999, but it is better to just remember 112, as it is more widely used now. There is a little confusion over whether to promote 112 or 999 in schools, but they both work equally well. If there is a very serious accident, call 112 (or 999) to get either an ambulance or the fire brigade.

Pizza Swirls

Ingredients:

Lukewarm water	200g strong white flour	1 tbsp oil
1 tsp sugar	1 sachet yeast	1 tsp salt
	Tomato purée	Grated cheese

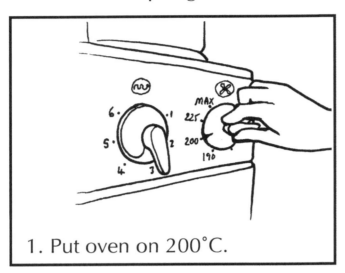

1. Put oven on 200°C.

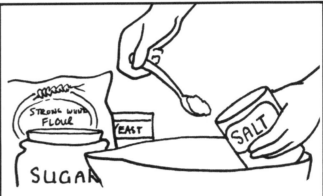

2. Put flour, yeast, salt, sugar and oil in a bowl.

3. Add enough lukewarm water to form dough.

4. Sprinkle work surface with flour and knead dough for 5–10 minutes.

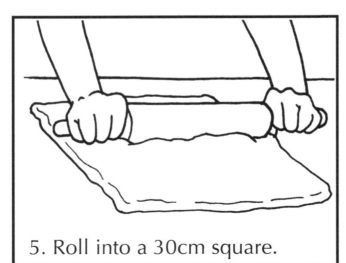

5. Roll into a 30cm square.

6. Spread tomato purée on dough.

Pizza Swirls (cont.)

Equipment: Mixing bowl   Cheese grater   Mixing spoon
Baking tray   Scales   Knife   Flour dredger
Rolling pin   Measuring spoons

7. Sprinkle grated cheese on top.

8. Roll up the dough.

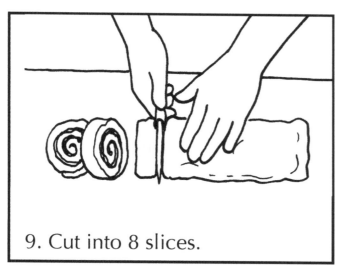

9. Cut into 8 slices.

10. Flatten the slices and put on baking tray.

11. Leave to rise if time.

12. Bake in the oven for 10–15 minutes.

Pizza Swirls

Ingredients:
200g strong white flour
1 tbsp oil
Lukewarm water
1 sachet yeast
1 tsp salt
1 tsp sugar
Tomato purée
Grated cheese

Equipment:
Mixing bowl
Cheese grater
Mixing spoon
Baking tray
Scales
Flour dredger
Rolling pin
Knife
Measuring spoons

Instructions:

1. Put oven on 200°C.

2. Put flour, yeast, salt, sugar and oil in a bowl.

3. Add enough lukewarm water to form dough.

4. Sprinkle work surface with flour and knead dough for 5–10 minutes.

5. Roll into a 30cm square.

6. Spread tomato purée on dough.

7. Sprinkle grated cheese on top.

8. Roll up the dough.

9. Cut into 8 slices.

10. Flatten the slices and put on a baking tray.

11. Leave to rise if time.

12. Bake in the oven for 10–15 minutes.

Guacamole

How to Cut an Avocado

You cut an avocado lengthwise, halfway through each side of the avocado. You can't cut all the way through as there is a stone in the middle. When you have cut all the way round, you twist the two halves and separate them. It can be a little hard to remove the stone, but the safest way is to scoop it out with a spoon. Watch a demonstration of how to get the flesh out. You will see that you can cut squares in the flesh whilst it is still in the peel. Then remove all the squares by scooping them out with a spoon.

When is an Avocado Ripe?

You can tell if an avocado is ripe by gently pressing it with your hand, particularly the area around the stalk. Hold it the same way that you would hold a remote control. The avocado should feel soft, but not too soft. If you buy an avocado that isn't ripe, just leave it for a couple of days to ripen up.

Knives Should be Sharp

Always cut using a knife with a sharp blade.

The safest knife is actually one that has a really sharp blade. This is because you do not need to put much effort into cutting something. If the blade is blunt you will probably be pressing harder and this is when the knife can slip and cause an accident.

Guacamole

Ingredients:

1 ripe avocado	½ lime	1 tsp fresh coriander
1 small shallot	Pinch of cayenne pepper	

1. Cut the avocado in half.

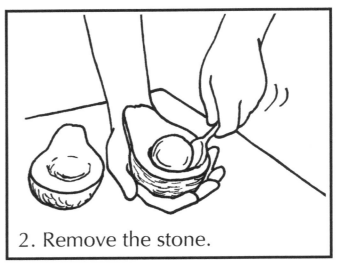

2. Remove the stone.

3. Cut the avocado flesh in small squares and scoop out.

4. Put avocado pieces in a bowl.

5. Squeeze lime juice with a lemon squeezer.

6. Add lime juice to bowl.

Guacamole (cont.)

Recipe

Equipment:

Sharp knife	Chopping board	Spoon
Mixing bowl	Lemon squeezer	Fork

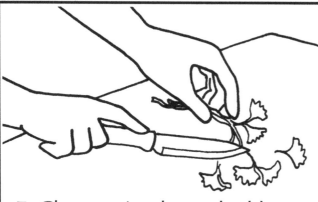

7. Chop coriander and add to bowl.

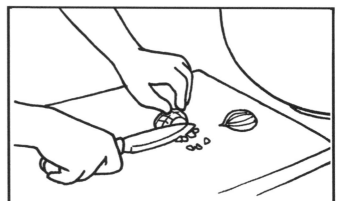

8. Chop the shallot and add to bowl.

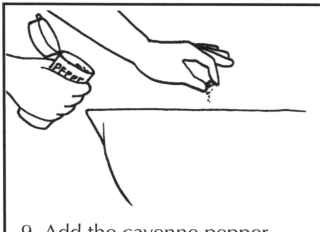

9. Add the cayenne pepper.

10. Mix it all well.

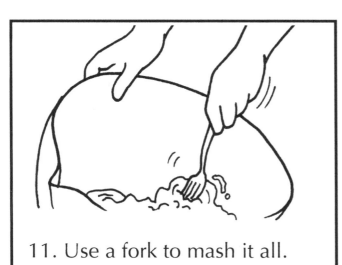

11. Use a fork to mash it all.

12. Serve as a dip.

Guacamole

Skill

Ingredients:
1 ripe avocado
½ lime
1 tsp fresh coriander
1 small shallot
Pinch of cayenne pepper

Equipment:
Sharp knife
Chopping board
Spoon
Mixing bowl
Lemon squeezer
Fork

Instructions:

1. Cut the avocado in half.

2. Remove the stone.

3. Cut the avocado flesh in small squares and scoop out.

4. Put avocado pieces in a bowl.

5. Squeeze lime juice with a lemon squeezer.

6. Add lime juice to bowl.

7. Chop coriander and add to bowl.

8. Chop the shallot and add to bowl.

9. Add the cayenne pepper.

10. Mix it all well.

11. Use a fork to mash it all.

12. Serve as a dip.

Mini Focaccia

How to Knead Olives into Dough

When you knead olives into dough, you simply start by spreading a few olives on the table. Then you start kneading the dough on top of the olives until they are kneaded into the dough. After that, you spread a few more olives and repeat the kneading. You carry on until all the olives have been kneaded into the dough.

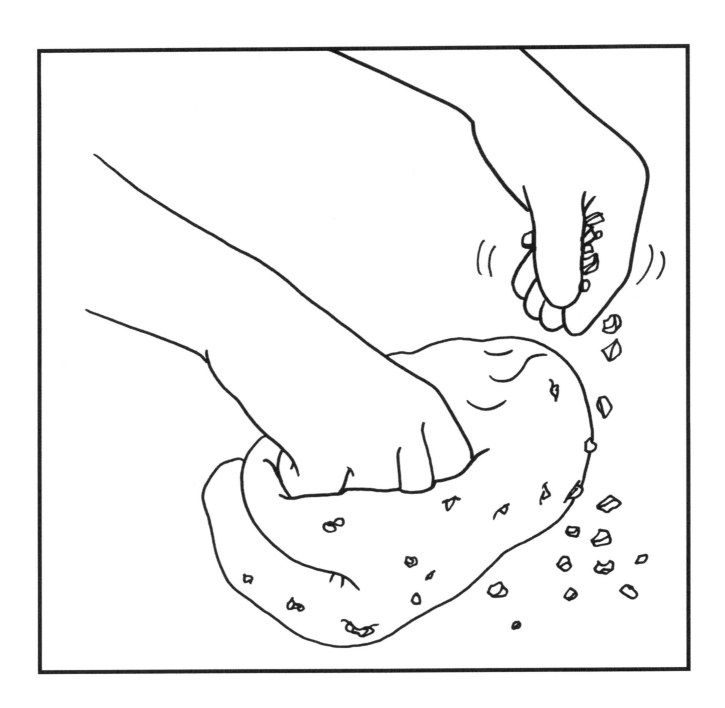

Monounsaturated Fat

Olive oil is a good source of monounsaturated fat.

Olive oil is very rich in monounsaturated fats. Studies suggest that monounsaturated fats can have a beneficial effect on your health when eaten in moderation and used to replace saturated fats or trans fats. The LDL cholesterol from saturated fats is also known as the "bad cholesterol", so by replacing these with monounsaturated fats, it can actually help reduce bad cholesterol levels in your blood which in turn leads to a lower risk of heart attacks and strokes. Monounsaturated fats also provide nutrients to help develop and maintain your body's cells. They are also typically high in vitamin E, an antioxidant vitamin.

Olive oil is a key ingredient in the Mediterranean diet. It is thought that this is why Mediterranean countries have lower levels of heart disease.

Put Knives Away After Use

When you have finished using a sharp knife and it is washed and dried, always return it to its place of storage straight away. If you do this as a matter of priority, you lessen the chance of accidents, accidents that can easily happen if sharp knives are just left lying around.

Mini Focaccia

Ingredients:

Lukewarm water

2–3 black olives

½ tsp salt

400g strong plain flour

3 sun-dried tomatoes

Coarse sea salt

4 tbsp olive oil

1 tsp caster sugar

2–3 stems rosemary

1 sachet yeast

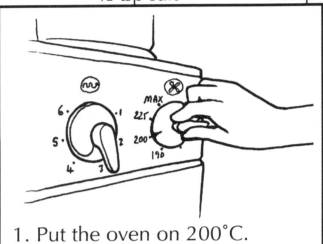

1. Put the oven on 200°C.

2. Put flour, yeast, sugar, salt and olive oil into bowl.

3. Add lukewarm water to form dough.

4. Knead the dough on a floured surface.

5. Cut the olives finely.

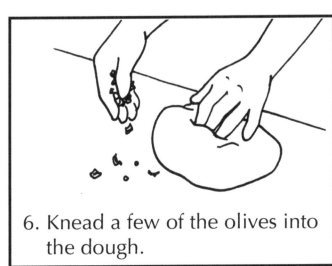

6. Knead a few of the olives into the dough.

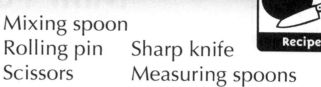

Equipment: Mixing bowl   Mixing spoon
Scales   Baking tray   Rolling pin   Sharp knife
Flour dredger   Chopping board   Scissors   Measuring spoons

7. Divide dough in two.

8. Pat each into an oval shape and put on a baking tray.

9. Make dents in each oval.

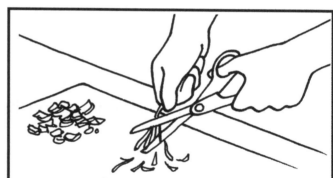

10. Cut the sun-dried tomatoes and rosemary with scissors. Press into holes.

11. Put olives and coarse salt on top. Pour a little olive oil over.

12. Bake in the oven for 15 minutes.

Teaching Healthy Cooking and Nutrition, Book 4

Mini Focaccia

Ingredients:
400g strong plain flour
1 sachet yeast
1 tsp caster sugar
½ tsp salt
4 tbsp olive oil
Lukewarm water
3 sun-dried tomatoes
A few stems rosemary
A few black olives
A little coarse sea salt

Equipment:
Mixing bowl
Mixing spoon
Scales
Baking tray
Rolling pin
Sharp knife
Flour dredger
Chopping board
Scissors
Measuring spoons

Instructions:

1. Put the oven on 200°C.

2. Put flour, yeast, sugar, salt and olive oil into bowl.

3. Add lukewarm water to form dough.

4. Knead the dough on a floured surface.

5. Cut the olives finely.

6. Knead a few of the olives into the dough.

7. Divide dough in two.

8. Pat each into an oval shape and put on a baking tray.

9. Make dents in each oval.

10. Cut the sun-dried tomatoes and rosemary with scissors. Press into holes.

11. Put olives and coarse salt on top. Pour a little olive oil over.

12. Bake in the oven for 15 minutes.

Leek and Mushroom Risotto

Skill

How to Simmer

Simmering is less vigorous than boiling. When a liquid is simmering, you can just see it bubbling gently. The skill is to keep the liquid at this temperature, not any hotter or any cooler. You may have to adjust the temperature controls on the hob to keep a liquid simmering.

How Do We Get Energy?

Theory

People need energy for everything they do: from walking to running to breathing and for our hearts to beat. Ultimately, all the energy we use comes from the Sun. Plants can get hold of this energy and store it in their seeds, stems, roots and tubers. We eat the plants, or we eat the animals that have eaten the plants. The food we eat is then broken down by our digestive system and taken around to different parts of our body. Basically, the energy from the Sun gets inside our bodies for us to use.

Freezers and Food

Health & Safety

A freezer should be below -18°C.

A freezer should run at -18°C. When food is frozen, the changes that lead to spoiling are slowed down. Bacteria, for example, cannot grow in the cold of the freezer. The bacteria are not actually killed; they are simply "dormant". Many types of food are quickly frozen in factories to maintain a high standard of freshness.

Leek and Mushroom Risotto

Ingredients:

4 mushrooms	1 leek	1 small onion	150g rice
500ml water	2 stock cubes	10g Parmesan	Olive oil

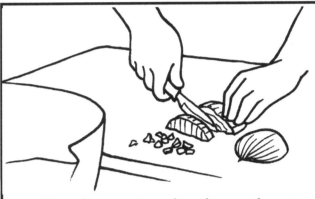

1. Cut the onion finely and put in a bowl.

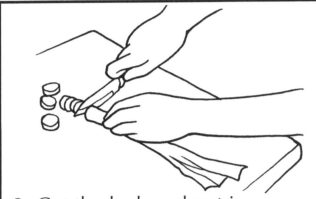

2. Cut the leek and put in another bowl.

3. Cut the mushrooms and add to the leek.

4. Prepare the stock.

5. Heat olive oil in a saucepan and fry the onion.

6. Add the rice and fry.

Leek and Mushroom Risotto (cont.)

Recipe

Equipment:

Chopping board   Sharp knife   2 mixing bowls
Mixing spoon   Measuring jug   Scales   Saucepan

7. Add the leek and mushrooms and continue to fry.

8. Pour a little of the stock over and simmer.

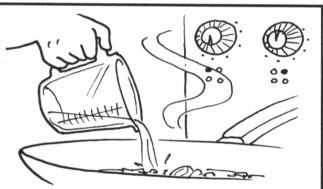

9. When the stock has been absorbed, add a little more.

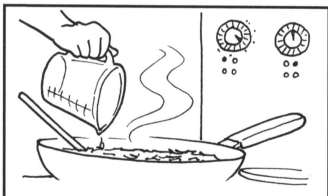

10. Keep adding stock until it has all gone (about 20 minutes).

11. Add the Parmesan.

12. Serve hot.

Teaching Healthy Cooking and Nutrition, Book 4

Leek and Mushroom Risotto

Ingredients:
4 mushrooms
1 leek
1 small onion
150g rice
500ml water
2 stock cubes
10g Parmesan
Olive oil

Equipment:
Chopping board
Sharp knife
2 mixing bowls
Mixing spoon
Measuring jug
Scales
Saucepan

Instructions:

1. Cut the onion finely and put in a bowl.

2. Cut the leek and put in another bowl.

3. Cut the mushrooms and add to the leek.

4. Prepare the stock.

5. Heat olive oil in a saucepan and fry the onion.

6. Add the rice and fry.

7. Add the leek and mushrooms and continue to fry.

8. Pour a little of the stock over and simmer.

9. When the stock has been absorbed, add a little more.

10. Keep adding stock until it has all gone (about 20 minutes).

11. Add the Parmesan.

12. Serve hot.

Corn Fritters

Skill

How to Turn Food over

Be very careful when you turn anything in a frying pan. This is because the hot oil can splash back and burn you. Get the turner under the fritter and tip it over gently yet firmly. Do not lift the fritter up in the air, but keep it well down. Always stand well back and watch what you are doing.

Measuring Energy in Food

We measure the energy in food in calories. A calorie is the same as 1 unit of energy. The number of calories in food basically tells us how much energy it contains. 1g of carbohydrates has 4 calories, 1g of protein has 4 calories and 1g of fat has 9 calories. As you can see, fat contains many more calories than carbohydrates or protein. Remember that we need to keep a balance between the number of calories we take in (food) and the number of calories we use (exercise). If we eat too many calories, we simply get fat.

Drying a Knife Safely

When you dry a knife, you start by holding the handle. Then you run the tea towel down the blade with the sharp edge pointing away from your hand. When you dry the handle, you have to hold the blade. Be very careful. Hold the sharp edge away from you. Then carry the knife safely and put it away immediately.

Corn Fritters

Ingredients:

150g tin of sweetcorn   200g plain flour   1 egg
½ tsp baking powder   Pinch of pepper   Oil
100g Cheddar cheese

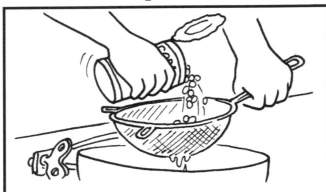

1. Open the tin of sweetcorn and drain it.

2. Crack the egg into a cup.

3. Beat it with a fork.

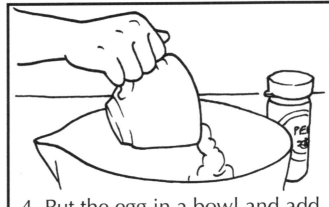

4. Put the egg in a bowl and add pepper.

5. Add the flour and mix.

6. Add the baking powder and mix.

Corn Fritters (cont.)

Equipment:

Tin opener	Cheese grater	Sieve	Frying pan
Scales	Turner	Fork	Teaspoon
Mixing bowl	Mixing spoon	Cup	Dessertspoon

7. Add the corn and mix.

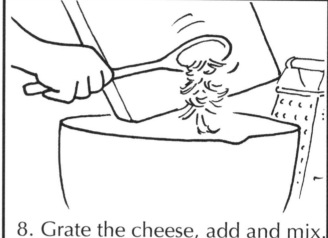

8. Grate the cheese, add and mix.

9. Heat a little oil in a frying pan.

10. Drop dessertspoons of mixture in the frying pan.

11. When golden, turn over and cook the other side.

12. Serve hot.

Teaching Healthy Cooking and Nutrition, Book 4

Corn Fritters

Ingredients:
150g tin of sweetcorn
200g plain flour
1 egg
½ tsp baking powder
Pinch of pepper
Oil
100g Cheddar cheese

Equipment:
Tin opener
Cheese grater
Sieve
Frying pan
Weighing scales
Turner
Fork

Teaspoon
Mixing bowl
Mixing spoon
Cup
Dessertspoon

Instructions:

1. Open the tin of sweetcorn and drain it.

2. Crack the egg into a cup.

3. Beat it with a fork.

4. Put the egg in a bowl and add pepper.

5. Add the flour and mix.

6. Add the baking powder and mix.

7. Add the corn and mix.

8. Grate the cheese, add and mix.

9. Heat a little oil in a frying pan.

10. Drop dessertspoons of mixture in the frying pan.

11. When golden, turn over and cook the other side.

12. Serve hot.

Onion Bhajis

How to Measure a Pinch

You measure a "pinch" between your thumb, index finger and middle finger. Basically, it means "a very small amount". It is often used in reference to measuring salt in a recipe.

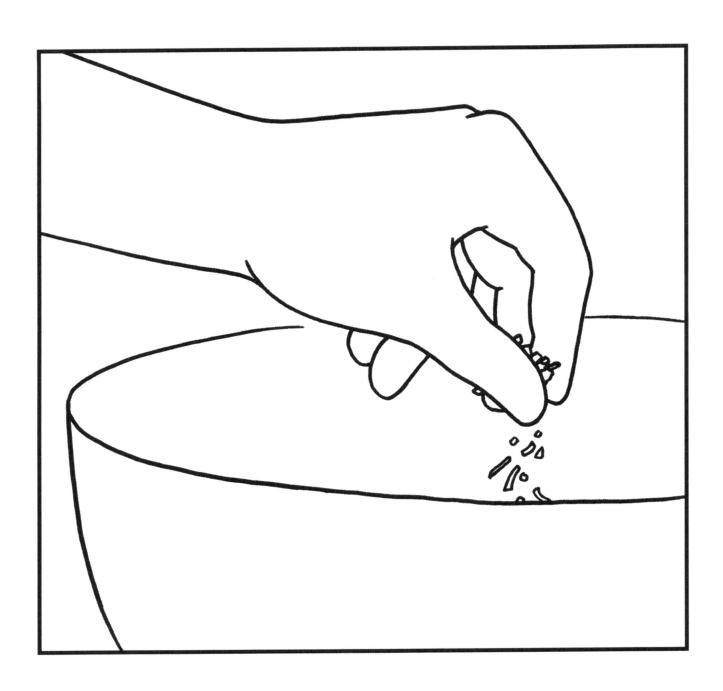

Why Does Chopping Onions Make Us Cry?

When you chop an onion, you often begin to cry. This is because certain enzymes escape when you cut through the cells of the onion. These enzymes set a chain reaction going, and in the end become a kind of gas. The gas reacts with the water in your eyes to produce a mild sulphuric acid, which irritates the eye. The brain then tells your tear ducts to produce more water to dilute this acid. This is why you begin to cry. The worst thing you can do is to rub your eyes with your hands, as these probably have onion juice all over them.

Fire Exits

Where are the fire exits?

You should always know where the nearest fire exits are, whether at school or at home. This is in case a fire occurs. You should also know where the fire assembly point is in your school. You should always know exactly what to do in case of a fire.

Onion Bhajis

Ingredients: 75g plain flour   Pinch of chilli powder
Pinch of turmeric   Fresh coriander   Pinch of cumin seeds
Pinch of onion seeds   1 onion   Cold water   Oil

1. Put flour in a mixing bowl.

2. Add the spices and mix well.

3. Chop the coriander finely.

4. Add coriander to bowl and mix.

5. Add the seeds and mix.

6. Chop the onion finely.

Onion Bhajis (cont.)

Recipe

Equipment:

Scales   Mixing bowl   Mixing spoon
Sharp knife   Frying pan   Chopping board
Measuring jug   Dessertspoon   Turner

7. Add to bowl and mix.

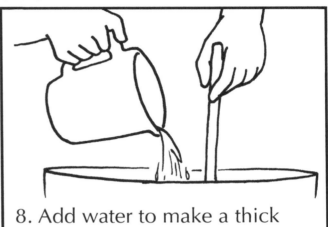

8. Add water to make a thick batter.

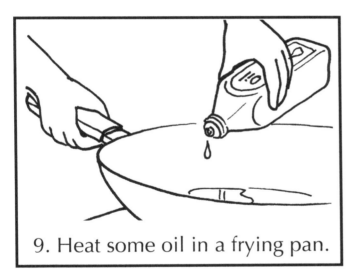

9. Heat some oil in a frying pan.

10. Drop dessertspoons of mixture in the hot pan.

11. Fry until golden, then turn over.

12. Serve hot.

Onion Bhajis

Recipe

Ingredients:
75g plain flour
Pinch of chilli powder
Pinch of turmeric
Fresh coriander
Pinch of cumin seeds
Pinch of onion seeds
1 onion
Cold water
Oil

Equipment:
Scales
Mixing bowl
Mixing spoon
Sharp knife
Frying pan
Chopping board
Measuring jug
Dessertspoon
Turner

Instructions:

1. Put flour in a mixing bowl.

2. Add the spices and mix well.

3. Chop the coriander finely.

4. Add coriander to bowl and mix.

5. Add the seeds and mix.

6. Chop the onion finely.

7. Add to bowl and mix.

8. Add water to make a thick batter.

9. Heat some oil in a frying pan.

10. Drop dessertspoons of mixture in the hot pan.

11. Fry until golden, and then turn over.

12. Serve hot.

Minestrone Soup

How to Sauté

When you sauté food, you fry it very quickly over a high heat while moving the food around with a turner. The word "sauté" comes from the French word "sauter", which means "to jump". This is because some chefs may shake the frying pan to move the food around. To do this is, of course, quite dangerous, so stick with using the turner until you have become a professional cook.

What is the Eatwell Plate?

The eatwell plate shows the types of food we need to eat, and how much of each type, to have a healthy and well-balanced diet. The plate is divided into five main food groups. Foods from the largest groups should be eaten most often and foods from the smallest group should be eaten least often. We need a balance of different types of food to get all the essential nutrients our bodies need to be healthy and function efficiently.

For further information, go to www.nhs.uk/Livewell/Goodfood/Pages/eatwell-plate.aspx

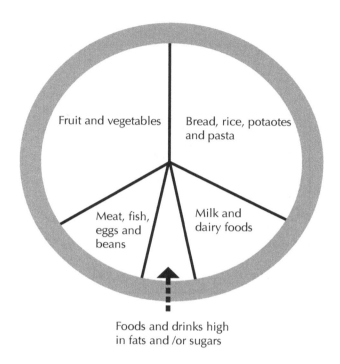

Fruit and vegetables

Bread, rice, potaotes and pasta

Meat, fish, eggs and beans

Milk and dairy foods

Foods and drinks high in fats and /or sugars

If YOU Catch on Fire

Stop, drop and roll.

If your clothes or your hair have caught fire, you must "Stop, drop and roll". This is a way of putting out the fire. You must first STOP so that you do not fan the fire and make it worse, and so that others can help you put out the fire. Then you must DROP and ROLL. This is to put the fire out by depriving it of oxygen. If there is a rug nearby, you can roll yourself in it to stop the fire. If there is a fire blanket, others can wrap this around you. The worst thing you can do is panic, so know what to do before the accident happens.

Minestrone Soup

Ingredients: 1 tbsp olive oil 500ml water 1 clove garlic
½ tin tomatoes 1 small onion 1 small carrot 2 stock cubes
½ leek 1 small parsnip 1 dsp tomato purée 1 handful soup pasta

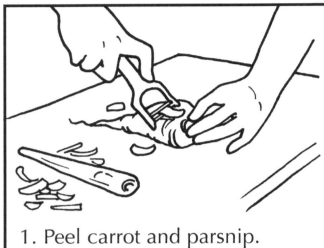

1. Peel carrot and parsnip.

2. Chop the carrot and parsnip and put in a bowl.

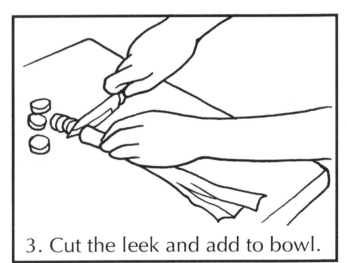

3. Cut the leek and add to bowl.

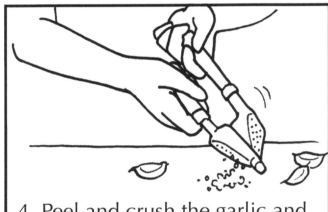

4. Peel and crush the garlic and add to bowl.

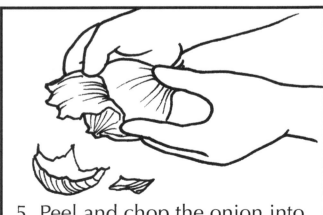

5. Peel and chop the onion into small cubes.

6. Heat the oil in a frying pan.

Minestrone Soup (cont.)

Equipment: Mixing bowl   Peeler   Chopping board
Sharp knife   Tin opener   Turner   Measuring jug
Frying pan   Garlic crusher   Dessertspoon

Recipe

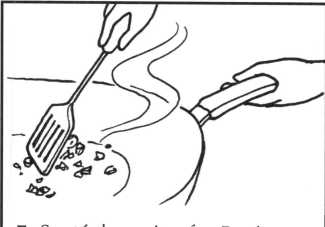

7. Sauté the onion for 5 minutes.

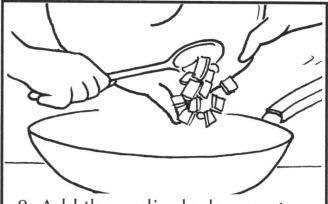

8. Add the garlic, leek, carrot and parsnip and sauté.

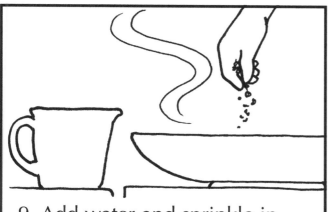

9. Add water and sprinkle in stock cubes

10. Add the tomatoes and tomato purée and mix.

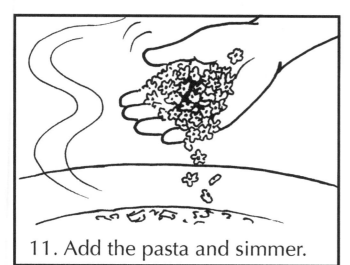

11. Add the pasta and simmer.

12. Serve when ready.

Teaching Healthy Cooking and Nutrition, Book 4

Minestrone Soup

Ingredients:
1 tbsp olive oil
500ml water
1 clove garlic
½ tin tomatoes
1 small onion
1 small carrot
2 stock cubes
½ leek
1 small parsnip
1 dsp tomato purée
1 handful soup pasta

Equipment:
Mixing bowl
Peeler
Chopping board
Sharp knife
Tin opener
Turner
Measuring jug
Frying pan
Garlic crusher
Dessertspoon

Instructions:

1.   Peel carrot and parsnip.

2.   Chop the carrot and parsnip and put in a bowl.

3.   Cut the leek and add to bowl.

4.   Peel and crush the garlic and add to bowl.

5.   Peel and chop the onion in small cubes.

6.   Heat the oil in a frying pan.

7.   Sauté the onion for 5 minutes.

8.   Add the garlic, leek, carrot and parsnip and sauté.

9.   Add water and sprinkle in stock cubes.

10.   Add the tomatoes and tomato purée and mix.

11.   Add the pasta and simmer.

12.   Serve when ready.

TIP
Share one tin of tomatoes between two sets of partners.

Chilli con Carne

Skill

How to Open a Tin

Be very careful when you open a tin with a tin opener, as the sharp edge can cut you. There are many types of tin openers. The most common one is the butterfly tin opener. With this type of tin opener, you have to press a sharp part into the tin, hold the tin opener very firmly with one hand and turn the butterfly handle with the other hand. The danger is that if you do not hold the tin opener firmly enough, it could slip and you could cut yourself on the tin.

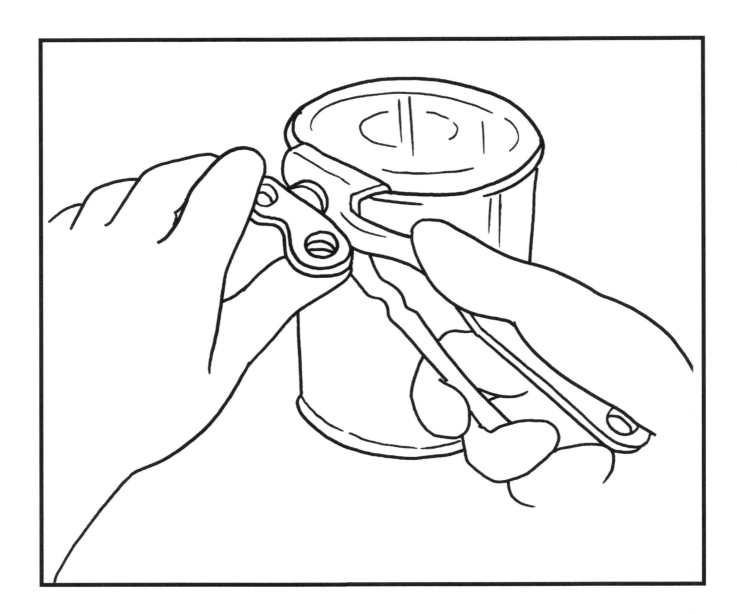

What is a Balanced Diet?

A balanced diet means that you eat some food from each food group on a regular basis. This is because the different foods have different nutrients that are needed regularly for the body. The eatwell plate illustrates which foods you need most of and which you need least of.

You don't need to get this balance right for every meal, but you should aim to get it over a longer period of time, such as every day or every week.

Preserving Food

You can preserve food by canning it.

Canning is a method of preserving food by sealing it in an airtight container such as the tin used for baked beans or tomatoes. The food inside the tin is then heated to destroy any micro-organisms that would otherwise spoil the food. This method of preserving will keep the food for a long time.

Recipe

Chilli con Carne

Ingredients: 125g lean minced meat   1 bay leaf
1 onion   ½ tin of baked beans   1 parsnip
1 carrot   1 stock cube   ½ tin of tomatoes   1 tsp chilli powder

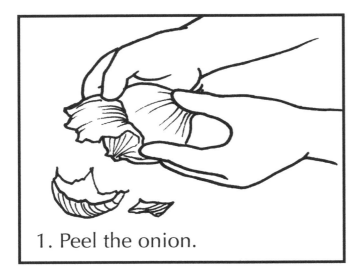

1. Peel the onion.

2. Chop the onion finely.

3. Peel and grate the carrot.

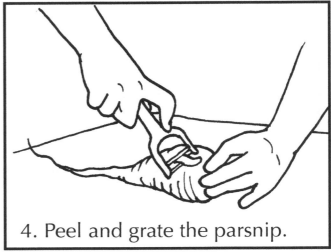

4. Peel and grate the parsnip.

5. Open the tin of tomatoes.

6. Heat a little oil in a frying pan.

Chilli con Carne (cont.)

Recipe

Equipment:

Chopping board   Sharp knife   Peeler   Grater

Tin opener   Frying pan   Turner

7. Fry the onion.

8. Add the minced meat and fry.

9. Add the carrot and parsnip.

10. Add the tomatoes, chilli powder and bay leaf. Simmer for 15 minutes.

11. Add the baked beans and simmer for 2 minutes.

12. Serve with rice.

Teaching Healthy Cooking and Nutrition, Book 4

Chilli con Carne

Ingredients:
125g lean minced meat
1 bay leaf
1 onion
½ tin of baked beans
1 parsnip
1 carrot
1 stock cube
½ tin of tomatoes
1 tsp chilli powder

Equipment:
Chopping board
Sharp knife
Peeler
Grater
Tin opener
Frying pan
Turner

Instructions:

1. Peel the onion.

2. Chop the onion finely.

3. Peel and grate the carrot.

4. Peel and grate the parsnip.

5. Open the tin of tomatoes.

6. Heat a little oil in a frying pan.

7. Fry the onion.

8. Add the minced meat and fry.

9. Add the carrot and parsnip.

10. Add the tomatoes, chilli powder and bay leaf. Simmer for 15 minutes.

11. Add the baked beans and simmer for 2 minutes.

12. Serve with rice.

What Can You Remember? (1)

Take this quiz after lesson 6.

1. Which letter is used for EU-recognized additives?

    E   X   W

2. What does a vegetarian eat?

    Only meat   No meat   A little meat

3. Which nutrient do vegetarians particularly need to replace?

    Carbohydrates   Vitamins   Protein

4. Why do apples go brown when cut?

    Enzymes react with   Enzymes react with   Enzymes die
    oxygen   sunlight

5. How can you avoid apples going brown when cut?

    Look at them   Add lemon juice   Blow on them

6. Why are edible mushrooms good for you?

    They're high in fat   They're low in fat   They attract fairies

7. How do you kill micro-organisms in food?

    Cool it   Wrap it up   Cook thoroughly

8. Why is strong flour good for bread making?

    It can lift heavy furniture   It contains a lot of   It can do push-ups
                                             gluten

9. What is the emergency number used in all EU countries?

    123   321   112

10. How do you know that an avocado is ripe?

    It feels soft   It feels hard   It feels prickly

Name _____ Date _____ Score _____

What Can You Remember? (2)

Take this quiz after lesson 12.

1. What type of fat does olive oil have a lot of?

    Butter   Monounsaturated   Saturated

2. Where does all energy ultimately come from?

    The Moon   The Earth   The Sun

3. What temperature should the freezer be at?

    -18°C   18°C   180°C

4. How do we measure energy in food?

    In calories   With scales   With a ruler

5. Why do we cry when we chop onions?

    It is very sad   They are tears of joy   It creates a gas

6. What does the eatwell plate show?

    Food groups   A Pharaoh   Tutankamun

7. What nutrient do you find in the Bread, Cereal, Rice and Pasta group?

    Fat   Carbohydrates   Vitamin C

8. What should you do if your clothes catch fire?

    Stop, drop and roll   Panic and run away   Nothing

9. How can you best describe an unopened tin?

    Full of bacteria   Pretty   Airtight

10. What happens when the food is safely inside a can?

    It is heated   It is cooled   It is put in water

Name _____ Date _____ Score _____

Certificate of Achievement

Teaching Healthy Cooking and Nutrition, Book 4

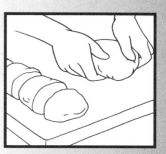

Name

_____

Is Able to

Shape Rolls

Use a Brush

Core an Apple

Use Measurements on
Packaging

Flatten Slices

Cut an Avocado

Knead Olives
into Dough

Simmer

Turn Food Over

Measure a Pinch

Sauté

Open a Tin

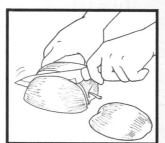

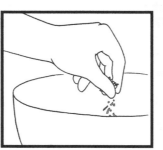

Allergy/lifestyle/religious considerations

The chart below lists possible substitutions that can be made (where possible) for children with common allergies/intolerances and/or lifestyle/religious considerations. It is not exhaustive and it is important to check with parents prior to doing any cooking activities.

Recipe	Possible substitutions
Cheesy Bread with Rosemary	This recipe is not suitable for children with gluten/wheat allergies. (Alternative gluten free recipes can be found on the Internet.) Lactose free hard cheese and margarine may be used for children who are lactose intolerant. Milk can be used to brush the tops of the buns instead of eggs for children who can't eat eggs.
Savoury Rolls	This recipe is not suitable for children with gluten/wheat and/or egg allergies.
Apple Crumble	For children with gluten/wheat allergies, gluten free flour and oats may be used. Dairy free margarine may be used for children who are lactose intolerant.
Cheese and Mushroom Tarts	This recipe is not suitable for children with gluten/wheat and/or egg allergies. Lactose free hard cheese, margarine and milk (eg rice or oat milk) may be used for children who are lactose intolerant.
Pizza Swirls	This recipe is not suitable for children with gluten/wheat allergies. Dairy free hard cheese may be used for children who are lactose intolerant.
Guacamole	None needed.
Mini Focaccia	This recipe is not suitable for children with gluten/wheat allergies.

Allergy/lifestyle/religious considerations (cont.)

Recipe	Possible substitutions
Leek and Mushroom Risotto	Use gluten free stock cubes for any children with a gluten intolerance. Some children may be unable to eat aged cheeses, such as Parmesan, either because they are lactose intolerant, or as they are sensitive to the histamines that are found naturally in these cheeses. Check with parents first.
Corn Fritters	This recipe is not suitable for children with egg allergies. Lactose free hard cheese may be used for children who are lactose intolerant. Replace the plain flour and baking powder with plain gluten free flour and baking powder for children who have gluten/wheat allergies.
Onion Bhajis	If you have children with gluten/wheat allergies, you can replace the plain flour with gram flour, which is made from ground chana dahl, a type of small chickpea.
Minestrone Soup	Use gluten free stock cubes and pasta for any children with a gluten intolerance.
Chilli con Carne	Use beef mince for children who don't eat pork due to lifestyle/religious considerations. Quorn can be used instead of mince for vegetarians. Use gluten free stock cubes for any children with a gluten intolerance. Also check that the baked beans are gluten free, as some brands contain gluten.